Contents

		page
1	Helping out	1
2	A better neighbourhood	8
3	Signs we see	15
4	Public transport	22
5	Catching a plane	29
6	Many years ago	36
7	Life in the past	43
8	The seasons of the year	50
9	Neighbours	57
10	A busy weekend	64
11	Special things we have done	71
12	Trees	78
13	Eating habits	85
14	A healthy meal	92
15	Places we visit	99
16	Our favourite TV programmes	106
17	Pocket money	113
18	Our hobbies	120

1 Helping out

A 🔊 Listen. The children are doing some jobs for their mothers. What are they doing at these places?

Sam is paying a bill at the bank.

1  buy stamps	2  return books	3  borrow books
4  buy take-away food	5  buy a newspaper	6  pay a bill

1 VOCABULARY

B Cherry is going to help her grandmother. What is she going to do?

Cherry is going to tidy the flat.
She is going to put the rubbish out.

Charlie wanted to help his grandmother too. What did he do? Where did he go?

> Please buy some oranges, some stamps, a newspaper and some take-away food. Can you also return my books and pay this bill? Thank you, Charlie.

First — LIBRARY
After that — BANK
Next — POST OFFICE
Then — NEWSAGENT
After that — SUPERMARKET
Lastly — RESTAURANT

First Charlie went to the library. He returned the books.
After that he went to the bank. He paid the bill.

D 🎧 **Listen and read. A treasure map.**

1 Mr and Mrs Green lived in a small town. They did not have much money. Mrs Green worked very hard but Mr Green never helped at home.

"Can you dig the garden for me? I want to plant some vegetables."

"Not now, dear. I'm going to meet my friend. I'll do it later."

2 When Mr Green came home, Mrs Green showed him an old box. Inside there was a treasure map.

"I found this today."

"Oh, it says there's some treasure in our garden. I know! I'll dig up the garden to find it."

3 Mr Green was not very clever. He did not know how to read maps.

"First I'm going to dig near the house."

4 When Mr Green stopped for lunch, he made a plan.

"Next I'm going to dig round the tree. After that I'll dig near the field."

What do you think Mr Green will find?

5 Mr Green dug and dug the garden. It was getting dark. He was tired and hot.

Bring me a light, dear. I'm going to dig the last part of the garden. I really want to find that treasure.

6

I didn't find any treasure.

Never mind, dear. Thank you for digging the garden. Now I can plant some lovely vegetables.

E **Put the sentences in the correct order.**

- [ ] **a** Mr Green did not find any treasure in the garden.
- [ ] **b** Mrs Green was happy. She could plant some vegetables.
- [ ] **c** Then he dug round the tree.
- [ ] **d** He started digging near the house.
- [ ] **e** After that he dug near the field. Finally he dug the last part of the garden in the dark.
- [1] **f** Mrs Green wanted to plant some vegetables but her husband did not want to help her.
- [ ] **g** Mrs Green showed Mr Green a treasure map. Mr Green wanted to find the treasure in the garden.

F Today is a school holiday. Peter is going to help his mother. Ask and answer questions.

Reading. The helpful husband.

One day, Mrs Jones woke up feeling sick. Her face was a funny colour, and she couldn't stop sneezing! 'A-SHOO!' A-SHOO!'

At breakfast, she told her husband, 'I'm going to see the doctor.' Mr Jones said, 'Can I do anything to help?'

Mrs Jones said, 'Can you do the shopping after work this evening? A-SHOO! I'll write a shopping list. A-SHOO! A-SHOO!'

Mr Jones drove to his office. After work, he came home. His wife was asleep in the bedroom, but Mr Jones found a list on the kitchen table. He read the list, 'Flowers, cream, fish, duck, burgers, garlic, curry, strawberries and peanuts.' He thought, 'Why does she want peanuts? What is she going to do with a duck?'

First he went to the supermarket. After that he went to the flower shop. Lastly he bought a take-away curry.

When he got home, his wife was awake. She said, 'I feel better now and I'm not sneezing.' Then she saw the shopping. 'What's that?' she asked.

'I found the shopping list on the table, so I went and did the shopping,' Mr Jones said.

'Oh no!' his wife said. 'That wasn't a shopping list. It's a list from the doctor. He says I mustn't eat those things. And the flowers will make me sneeze. A-SHOO! A-SHOO!'

2 A better neighbourhood

A 🎧 Listen. This is Mary's neighbourhood. What places are there in her neighbourhood?

There is a sports centre.
There are public toilets.

VOCABULARY 8

B Sally is visiting Mary. She is asking Mary about the public facilities in her neighbourhood. Ask and answer.

1. a dental clinic? ✓  go to the dentist
2. recycling bins? ✗  recycle rubbish
3. a library? ✗  borrow books
4. a swimming pool? ✗  go swimming
5. postboxes? ✓ post a letter

Is there a dental clinic in your neighbourhood?

Yes, there is. We can go to the dentist here.

Are there recycling bins?

No, there aren't. We can't recycle rubbish here.

LANGUAGE FOCUS

C Sally and her family are looking at a model of their new neighbourhood. What do they need? Make sentences.

There isn't a playground. We can't play outside.

There isn't a post office. We can't send a parcel.

✗ library / borrow books

✗ clinic / go to the doctor

✗ car park / park our car

We need a playground.

We need a car park.

_____
_____
_____

D 🎧 **Listen and read. No place like home.**

1. Paul lived in a small village. The village was old but he was happy there. He had a lot of good friends at the village school.

   One day there was a fire and Paul's house burned down.

Now we'll have to move.

Don't worry, Paul. You'll get a nice new home in a different neighbourhood.

2. Paul's family found a new home in a town nearby. After he moved, Paul invited his friends from the village school to visit him.

How do you like your neighbourhood?

It's very nice. There's a market and a shopping centre.

There's also a train station and a library. We're very happy in our new neighbourhood.

3 Paul did not say anything.

What's the matter, Paul? Don't you like your new neighbourhood?

I'd love to live here. There's a cinema and a sports centre.

It's very nice but there's no place like my old home. I don't know anyone here. It'll take me a long time to make friends at my new school. I miss you all very much.

Do you understand how Paul felt?

E   Answer the questions about the story.

1   Where was Paul's old home?
2   Why did Paul like his old home?
3   What happened to Paul's old home?
4   Where was Paul's new home?
5   What places are there in Paul's new neighbourhood?
6   Why was Paul unhappy in his new neighbourhood?

Here is Paul's new address.   **Now write your own address here.**

Start with the **SMALLEST** place.

Paul Young
Flat 26
Palace Street
Vancouver
Canada

End with the **BIGGEST** place.

F Sally's father, Mr Black, is having a meeting with the Neighbourhood Committee. Make sentences.

There's a swimming pool. We can go swimming.

There isn't a clinic. We can't go to the doctor. We need a clinic.

swimming pool	✓
clinic	✗
car park	✗
library	✗
post office	✗
playground	✗

After the meeting, Mr Black wrote a letter to the government.

1 Write your address and the date here.

2 Write the name of the person here. Write 'Sir/Madam' if you do not know his/her name.

3 Write a paragraph about one main idea.

4 Write a paragraph about another idea.

5 Write an ending.

6 Write your name and who you are.

Flat 23
163 White Street
London
United Kingdom

17th September 2005

Dear Sir/Madam,

We need a clinic and a car park. We cannot go to the doctor or park our cars in the neighbourhood.

We hope you will give us a clinic and a new car park soon. We need a better neighbourhood.

Yours faithfully,
Jack Black

Chairman
Neighbourhood Committee

Reading. A letter from London.

Hanan is from Cairo, but she and her family are living in London for a year. This letter is from Hanan to her friend in Cairo.

Dear Samia,

Thank you for your letter. I enjoyed reading it because I miss my friends. But London is exciting, and the people at my new school are nice.

My teacher says I must practise my English. That's why I'm writing to you in English. My teacher helped me.

A lot of things are different here. The weather is cold and it often rains. I need an umbrella but I haven't got one yet, so I often get wet! The weekend is different, it's on Saturday and Sunday, not Friday. The buses are different, they are red and they have two floors. I like riding on the top floor.

Our neighbourhood is OK. Near our house, there is a big park with lots of green grass, trees, water and a really good playground. I can go there after school.

Last weekend, I went on the London Eye with my parents. That was great! The London Eye looks like a big bicycle wheel. In fact it's the biggest wheel in the world. We went into a big glass box and the wheel lifted us up high. We could see all of London from the top.

Write again soon.
Love from Hanan

3 Signs we see

A Listen. What signs can you see?

There is a 'No smoking' sign.
There is a 'Metro' sign.

1.
a 'No smoking' sign

2.
a 'Metro' sign

3.
a 'Sale' sign

4.
an 'Open' sign

5.
a 'Closed' sign

6.
a 'Wet floor' sign

B Here are some of the signs we see in the street. Find these signs in the picture.

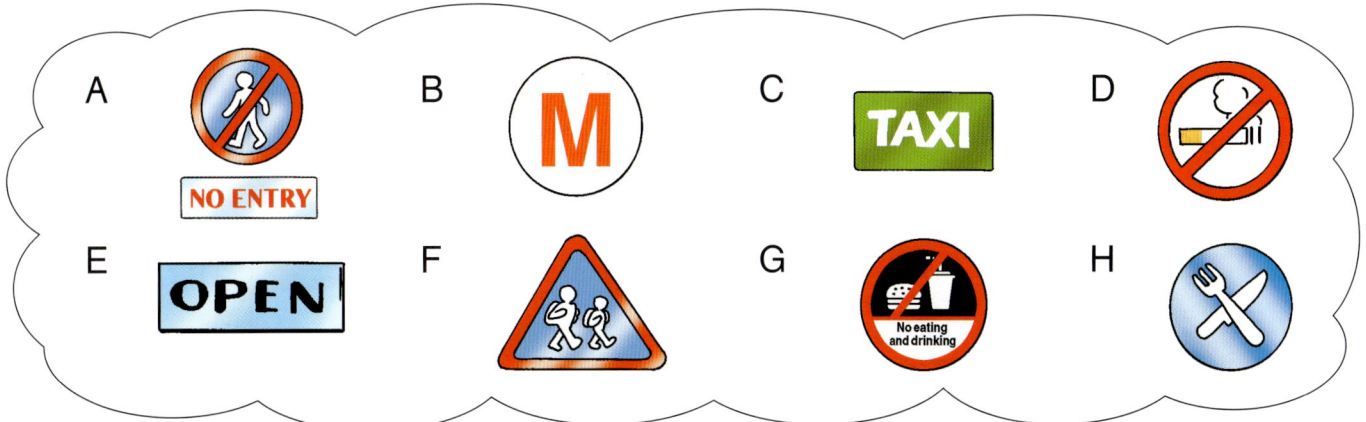

We see Sign A on a door.
We see Sign B above a Metro station.
We see Sign C beside a road.
We see Sign D at a restaurant.

C Betty's little brother cannot read. Betty is explaining what the signs mean. Complete the sentences.

must   mustn't   can

Some signs tell us rules.   Some signs give us information.

1
It says 'Silence'.
It means 'You mustn't talk.'

2
It says 'Exit'. It means 'You can go out here.'

3
It says 'Save energy'. It means 'You _____ turn off the lights when you leave.'

4
It says 'Sale'. It means 'You _____ buy things at a lower price.'

5
It says 'No food'. It means 'You _____ bring food in here.'

6
It says 'Taxi'. It means 'You _____ take a taxi here.'

D Listen and read. A bad start.

1. Mrs Smith wanted to open her new shop but the signs were not ready. She asked Bob to help her.

2. Bob went to the shop at seven o'clock. He put up all the signs.

3. Then he opened the shop.

4 Nobody came to the shop all day. At six o'clock Bob went into the street. He asked a boy to come in.

5 Joyful Toy Shop did not have a good start. It made no money all day.

E   Are these sentences true or false? Put a ✔ or a ✘.

1 ☐ Mrs Smith did not open the shop.

2 ☐ Bob was the shopkeeper on the first day.

3 ☐ Bob put an 'Entrance' sign on the outside of the door.

4 ☐ Bob had to change the signs.

5 ☐ Bob was clever.

6 ☐ Joyful Toy Shop did not make any money on the first day.

F Here are some signs you can see in the street. Talk about the signs.

must	walk carefully	eat or drink	smoke here
mustn't	go into the shop	go in here	go out here
can	buy things at a lower price		
beside a road / door	on / above a door	at a shop / restaurant / toilet	on the Metro / train

This sign says 'Wet Floor'.
It means 'You must walk carefully.'
We see it at a public toilet.

1.
2.
3.
4.
5.
6.
7.

Reading. Silly signs.

My little brother and I went to a safari park last year. A safari park is like a zoo, but the animals are not in cages. They can walk anywhere inside the park. There are monkeys, deers, giraffes, elephants and many other animals. Our parents drove us through the park in the car. Some of the animals came very near. My parents said, 'You mustn't get out of the car.' I took lots of pictures. It was great!

At the entrance, there was a funny sign. It was funny because there was a mistake on it. The sign said, 'Elephants Please Stay in Your Car'. My little brother said, 'But elephants don't drive cars!' I said, 'It means elephants can be dangerous, so we must stay in our car.'

Can you correct the mistake in the sign?

I saw another funny sign outside the restaurant. The sign said, 'Open seven days a week and weekends.' I'm sure you can correct that one!

Then last week, I saw a funny sign in a shop window. In the shop, I could see pictures of famous places, like Paris, Rome, Athens, Dubai, Cairo and New York. The shop sells holidays to these places. There was a big sign in the window. The sign said, 'Go away!'

I think the sign means 'Go away on holiday', but it's not polite if you just say 'Go away!'

4 Public transport

  Listen. Talk about the different kinds of public transport.

a bus

the Metro

a train

a tram

a taxi

a ferry

Travelling by bus is uncomfortable.
Buses are crowded.

comfortable   uncomfortable

crowded   not crowded

cheap   expensive

VOCABULARY 22

B The children are talking about how they come to school. Make sentences.

1

I live near the tram line **so** I come to school by tram.

I live near the school **so** I walk to school.

The children are comparing different ways of coming to school. Make sentences.

2

Although travelling by tram is cheap, it's slow.

Walking to school is slow **but** it's free.

fast / uncomfortable

comfortable / expensive

Tell your friends what public transport YOU take to school.

 These people take public transport every day. What do they think about it? Make sentences.

1 read

I enjoy reading **on** the train.

2 stand

I hate standing **on** the Metro.

3 see litter

I don't like seeing litter **on** the bus.

4 sleep

I like _____ **in** the taxi.

5 look at the view

I enjoy _____ _____ **on** the ferry.

6 get on and off

I don't like _____ _____ the tram.

D Listen to this poem.

Public Transport

Millions of motor cars
Poison all the streets.
Millions of people,
Passengers in seats.

Thousands of trembling trains
Thunder down the track,
Underground, overground,
Into them we pack.

Hundreds of ferry boats
Flash across the sea,
Ferrying all the people,
Queuing on the quay.

Dozens of aeroplanes
Glide across the sky,
Touching down, taking off,
'Hello there!' 'Goodbye!'

by Mike Murphy

Read the poem.

E Answer the questions.

1. What do we call the people who travel by car or public transport?
2. Find a word that describes the noise the train makes.
3. What do we call the underground train?
4. What do ferry boats cross?
5. Find a word that means 'waiting in line'.
6. What do the words 'millions', 'thousands', 'hundreds' and 'dozens' tell you about transport? Do you agree with the poet?

Skills Read these sentences. Look at the words in blue.

1. I take the Metro to school every morning because it is fast.

2.  Travelling by tram is cheap but it is slow.

3. Buses are cool and comfortable. They are clean too.

4.  I feel sick on ferries so I don't like travelling on them.

Complete the sentences with one of the words in the box.

> they   them   it

1. Walking to school is slow but _____ is free.
2. I don't like standing on the Metro. _____ makes me tired.
3. Trams are crowded. I never go on _____.

F Beeno is telling the children about public transport on Mars. Finish what Beeno says. Then match the two parts of Beeno's sentences.

		spaceship	spacebug
1	fast	✓	✗
2	cheap	✗	✓
3	comfortable	✓	✗
4	crowded	✗	✓
5	hot	✗	✓
6	dirty	✗	✓

Travelling by spaceship is fast and comfortable. Travelling by spacebug is cheap, …

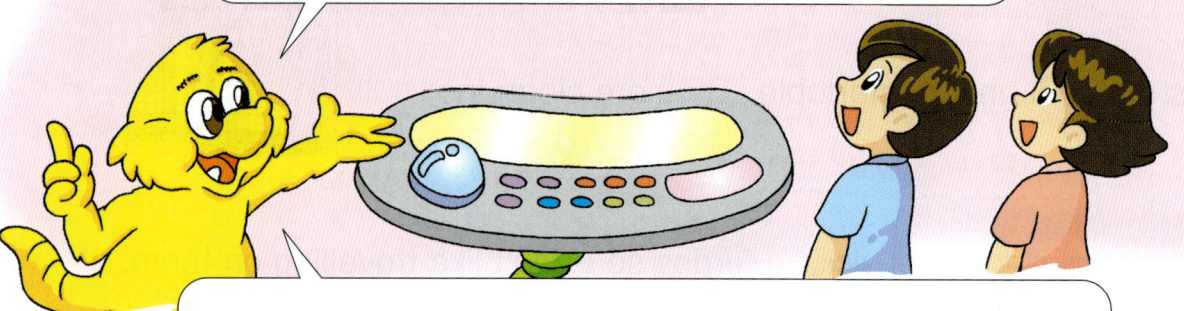

1 Travelling by spaceship is expensive ____
2 Travelling by spaceship is cool and clean so ____
3 Travelling by spacebug is cheap so ____
4 Although travelling by spacebug is uncomfortable, ____

(a) it's cheap.
(b) spacebugs are crowded.
(c) many people like travelling by spaceship.
(d) but it's comfortable.

Reading. Cars: past, present and future.

The story of cars is more than 120 years old. The first person to make a car was a German called Carl Benz. He finished his first car in 1885. His car had only three wheels and it was not very fast. It was slower than a horse.

Although that first car was uncomfortable and not very useful, it was very important because it started something new. After that, people in Germany and Britain made better cars. In 1900, cars had four wheels, they were bigger and more comfortable and they could go faster than a horse.

However, buying a car was very expensive. So travelling by car was only for very rich people. That changed in 1910. In that year, Henry Ford, an American, started making cheaper cars. They were not big and comfortable but they were cheap, so millions of people could buy them and enjoy travelling by car.

Now, cars are everywhere. We need cars. They are good for us, but they are also bad for us because they poison the streets. Some people drive badly, which is dangerous. Cars hit and kill thousands of people every year.

In the future, there will be more cars and more roads. So car-makers must make safer cars. Some scientists think computers will drive cars in the future. Then cars will be less dangerous.

5 Catching a plane

A Listen. The people are catching the plane. Where are they? What have they got?

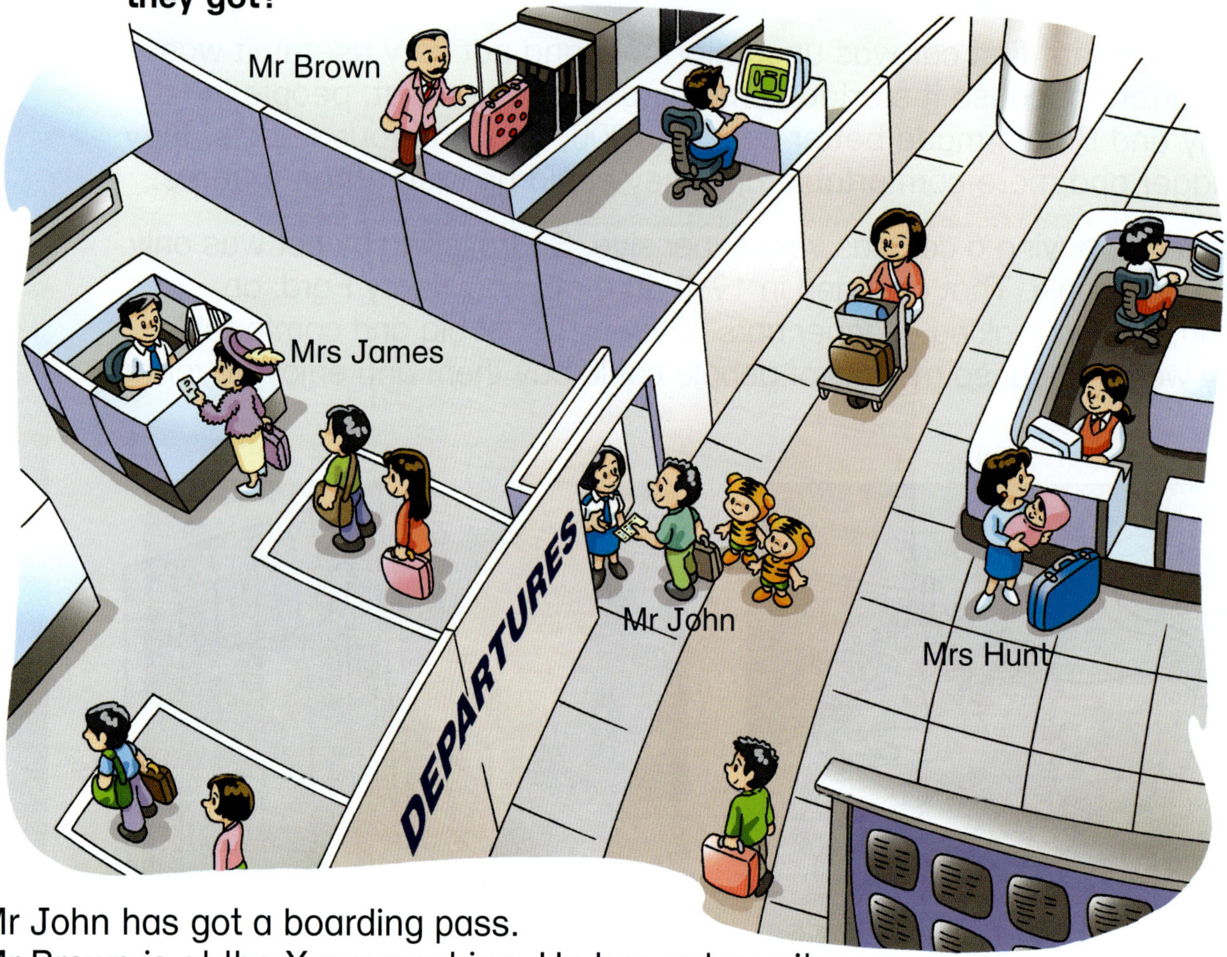

Mr John has got a boarding pass.
Mr Brown is at the X-ray machine. He has got a suitcase.

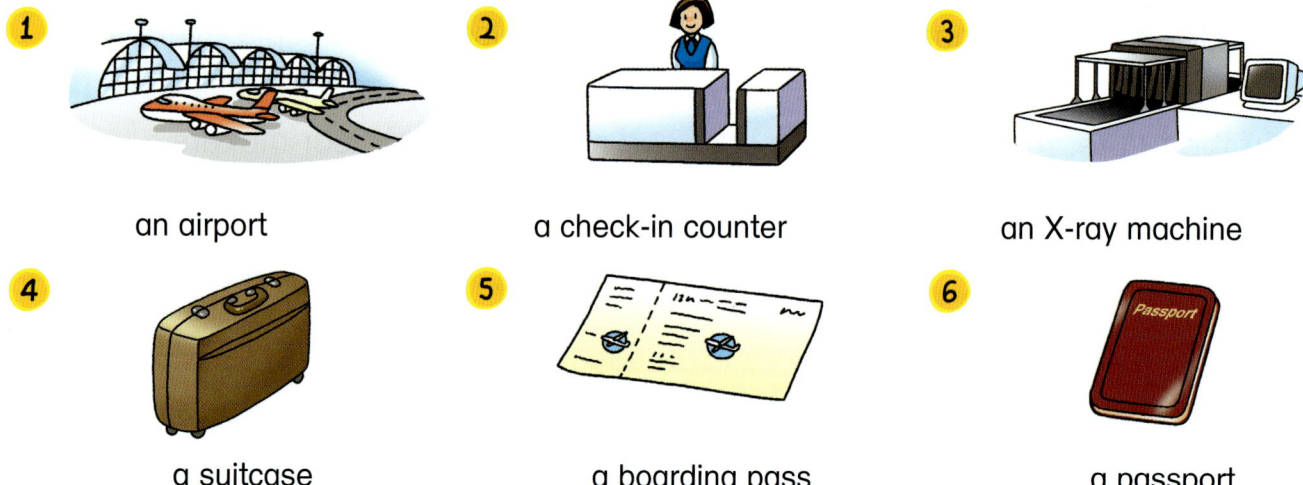

1. an airport
2. a check-in counter
3. an X-ray machine
4. a suitcase
5. a boarding pass
6. a passport

B The Johnsons are going on a trip. Make sentences.

We check in at the Airport Express station.
Then we take the train to the airport.
We show our passports.
Then we put our bags in the X-ray machine.
We show our boarding passes.
Then we get on the plane.

Now listen to Charlie.

We check in at the Airport Express station **before** we take the train to the airport.

We put our bags in the X-ray machine **after** we show our passports.

The Johnson family are on the plane. They sit in the wrong seats. Complete the sentences.

my   your   his   her   their   our

1

Excuse me, sir. These are not your seats. These are their seats. May I see your boarding passes, please?

Oh, sorry. Where are our seats?

2

Are those _____ seats?

No, sir. Those are _____ seats.

3

These are _____ seats, sir.

Thank you.

4

This is _____ seat and that's your seat, dear.

5

Is this Cherry's seat?

No, that's _____ seat.

6

Is this Charlie's seat?

Yes, it's _____ seat.

D 🎧 **Listen and read. An adventure at the airport.**

1. The Johnsons were at the airport. They were going to Australia on holiday. Charlie and Cherry saw two men with an interesting case.

2.

The plane landed at Sydney Airport. The two men got up and opened the locker. They were in a hurry to get off.

3.

At the airport, Charlie and Cherry waited for their suitcases to come off the plane. They saw the police checking all the bags carefully.

What do you think is in the men's case?

4   The two men left their case and walked quickly towards the exit.

5   As the two men were going out of the door, Cherry ran after them with their case.

E   **Match the two halves of the sentences about the story.**

1   The Johnsons were ____.

2   At the check-in counter Charlie and Cherry saw ____.

3   The men got up before ____.

4   At Sydney Airport the Johnsons saw ____.

5   Cherry picked up the men's case and ____.

6   The police stopped the men because ____.

(a) two police officers

(b) ran after them

(c) two men with an interesting case

(d) they had stolen jewellery in their case

(e) going on holiday to Australia

(f) the plane stopped moving

We got on the plane. We found ____ seats ____ we had a drink. Dad spilt ____ drink on Mum. We watched a film ____ we had a meal. Cherry did not want ____ meal so I ate it. I played video games ____ I went to sleep.

before   after   his   her   our

Reading. Our first flight.

'We're going to fly in a plane tomorrow!' said Jack excitedly. His sister, Jessica, was not so happy. She was afraid of flying.

The next morning, their parents drove them to the airport before breakfast. They had a big breakfast after they checked in. Then they waited for half an hour before the plane was ready. 'Good morning' the air hostess said as they walked onto the plane. Jack sat by a window, and Jessica sat between Jack and her mother.

They waited again before the plane started to move. It went faster and faster. Then suddenly it went up. Jessica felt afraid but also excited.

After a few minutes, she looked out of Jack's window. She could see blue sky and clouds. But the clouds were not up above, they were down below! 'We're flying above the clouds!' she said. 'It's beautiful!'

She and Jack looked down through the clouds. They could see very small houses and thin lines. 'Those lines are roads,' Jack said.

After some time, an air hostess brought drinks. Then Jack and Jessica listened to music through headphones. Then they looked out of the window again and saw the blue sea a long way down. 'Look! A ship!' said Jessica.

They could see houses and cars. The cars and houses got bigger. Before they landed, Jack said. 'Don't be afraid.' But Jessica wasn't afraid. 'I love flying' she said.

6 Many years ago

A Listen. Talk about London then and now.

LONDON THEN

horse and carriage

steam train

low buildings

dial phone

LONDON NOW

cars and buses

electric train

tall buildings

mobile phones

There were horses and carriages in old London. Now there are lots of cars and buses. There were no electric trains in old London. Now all the trains are electric.

B Beeno is at the London Museum with Tom and Mary. Complete the sentences.

Look, Beeno!
A hundred years ago people got water from a well.
Fifty years ago they got water from a tap.

A hundred years ago people rode in _____ .

Fifty years ago they _____ on _____ .

_____ people used _____ to read in the evenings.

_____

D Listen and read. London Town.

The Romans came to Britain about two thousand years ago. They built the capital city in London by the River Thames, then built a wall around it. But the Romans went home and Saxons from north Europe sailed in and raided the city. The British Museum and the Museum of London have lots of things from Roman times.

Next came the French. The Norman King William defeated the English King Harold at the battle of Hastings in 1066. The new government of England spoke French and the English spoke different languages. They didn't speak the English we have today.

London grew quickly. In about 1078 the government began to build the Tower of London. First, the Tower was a terrible prison. Many enemies of the king were killed there. Nowadays the Tower holds jewels of the kings and queens of Britain. Visitors can go and see these jewels.

Visitors to the Tower of London also like to see the ravens. Ravens are big black birds. There are seven of them in the Tower. Nobody knows when they came or where they came from. There is a myth that if the ravens fly away the kingdom and tower will fall. That's why there is a Raven Master. He looks after them. He also cuts their feathers on one side so they can't fly away.

E Answer the questions.

1. When did the Romans come to Britain?
2. Where can you see things from Roman Britain?
3. What was the name of the Norman king who invaded Britain?
4. What language did the new rulers of Britain speak?
5. What was the Tower of London first used for?
6. Why are the ravens important?
7. Why is the job of Raven Master important?

Skills Read these paragraphs from a book about London in the old days. Tick (✓) one sentence to add more information.

1. The Romans built the city of London. They built the city on the banks of the River Thames.

    ☐ (a) The British Museum has lots of things from Roman times.

    ☐ (b) London is the capital city of Britain.

    ✓ (c) The Romans built a wall to defend London from raiders.

2. The Norman King William defeated the English King Harold. He defeated him at the battle of Hastings.

    ☐ (a) Hastings is in the south of England.

    ☐ (b) The battle of Hastings was in 1066.

    ☐ (c) After the Romans went home, the Saxons raided London.

3. There are seven ravens in the Tower of London. They are big, black birds.

    ☐ (a) A man called a Raven Master looks after the ravens.

    ☐ (b) Ravens make a terrible noise.

    ☐ (c) The ravens can't fly away from the Tower of London.

F Act Professor Davis and the children.

1. This is Professor Davis. He wrote a book about London eighty years ago.

   Do you have any questions about my book, children?

2. Were there any houses in London eighty years ago?

   Yes, there were lots of houses.

   Were there any mobile phones?

   Oh, no. There were no mobile phones.

3. Did people travel by horse and carriage?

   No, they didn't. They travelled by bicycle.

   Did people watch colour TV?

   No, they didn't. There was no colour TV in those days, only black and white TV.

4. Did children play computer games?

   No, there were no home computers in those days.

Reading. Famous Londoners.

In London you can often see a blue plaque on the wall of a house. There is a name on the plaque. It is the name of a famous person who lived in the house in the past.

There are nearly 800 blue plaques in London. Some of the names are world famous. They are all people who did something important and useful.

Many of the people are famous inventors, such as John Logie Baird, the man who invented TV about 80 years ago. There is a blue plaque on the house where he showed the first TV in 1926. There are famous writers, such as Charles Dickens and Agatha Christie. There are people who have helped many other people, for example, Florence Nightingale. She started the first modern school for nurses more than 100 years ago. Before that, there were not many good hospitals because there were not many good nurses.

Not all the names on the plaques are British. For example, Mohammad Ali Jinnah was the leader of Pakistan when it was a new country in 1947. Before that, he worked in London for four years and was a student in London.

Some of the people are less famous but they are all interesting, for example, the first woman dentist and the greatest English clown.

Tourists and Londoners enjoy finding and reading the blue plaques. So now many cities in other countries have blue plaques. Are there some in your city?

7 Life in the past

A Listen. What can you see in the photos?

A girl is carrying water from the well.
They are living on a farm.

1.  get married
2.  live on a farm
3.  make clothes
4.  make cakes
5.  work in a field
6.  carry water

B Last week Sally visited an old ladies' home. She talked to Mrs Green. Ask questions.

1	**How many** children **did** your father **have**?	My father had five children.
2	**When did** you **get** married?	I got married when I was fifteen.
3	**Where did** you and your husband live?	We lived on a farm.
4	_____	Yes, we had two cats.
5	_____	Yes, there were a lot of mice on the farm.
6	_____	I made my own clothes in the evening.

Mrs Green and Mrs Lee are talking about their life when they were young. Make sentences.

D 🎧 Listen and read. The lion's promise.

1. Once upon a time a little monkey went for a walk in the forest. It passed a deep hole. A sad voice came from the hole.

2. The little monkey put its tail down the hole and pulled the lion out of the hole.

3.

4 Just then a tortoise came by. It saw the lion and the frightened monkey. It asked the monkey what was happening. The monkey started to tell the tortoise the story.

5 The lion let go of the monkey and got down in the hole. He waited for the monkey to pull him out.

E Answer the questions.

1. Where did the monkey go for a walk?
2. What did he see down in the hole?
3. What did the lion promise the monkey?
4. What did the lion say when the monkey got him out of the hole?
5. Who came along next?
6. Who went down into the hole?
7. What did the tortoise say to the monkey?

F Mr and Mrs Bates are telling Sally about life on their farm. Complete the sentences.

1

work / fields
drive / tractor

I worked in the fields.　I ... too.

I didn't ...　I ... either.

2

I planted vegetables and fed the animals.

When did you plant vegetables?
What vegetables ... plant?
When did you feed the animals?

in spring / potatoes and onions / every morning

3

I carried water from the well.

When ... water from the well?
What ... use to carry water?
How many buckets ... carry?

in the mornings and evenings / a bucket / two

Reading. Toys from the past.

Do you know what toys your parents played with? And your grandparents? What about your grandparents' grandparents? What about children who lived thousands of years ago?

One of the oldest toys in the world is a toy mouse from Egypt. It is about 4,000 years old, and now it is in a museum in London.

Do you play with marbles? Marbles are little balls made of glass. Egyptian children played with marbles too, but 5,000 years ago marbles were made of stone.

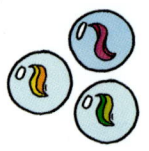

The Chinese learned how to fly kites 3,000 years ago. Soon after that, Greek children started playing with yo-yos. Can you use a yo-yo? The first picture of a yo-yo is 2,500 years old. The picture is on a bowl, and it shows a Greek boy playing with a yo-yo.

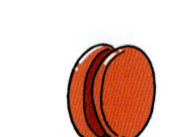

Most toys are not as old as marbles, kites and yo-yos. The last 300 years have been a busy time for inventors. For example, an inventor made the first pair of roller-skates in 1759. The first jigsaw puzzle came in 1767. In the 1800s people built the first playgrounds in parks. In 1856 a famous British scientist, Michael Faraday, invented rubber balloons.

Some inventions in the 1900s were electric trains, coloured pencils and toy cars. Computers were a very important invention, and the first computer games came out in the 1970s when your parents were young. They were very simple games, like video tennis, but they were exciting then because they were new.

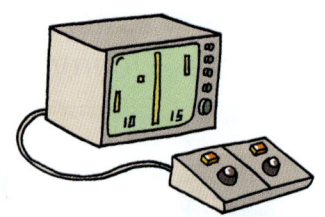

8 The seasons of the year

A  **Listen. Talk about the weather in these places.**

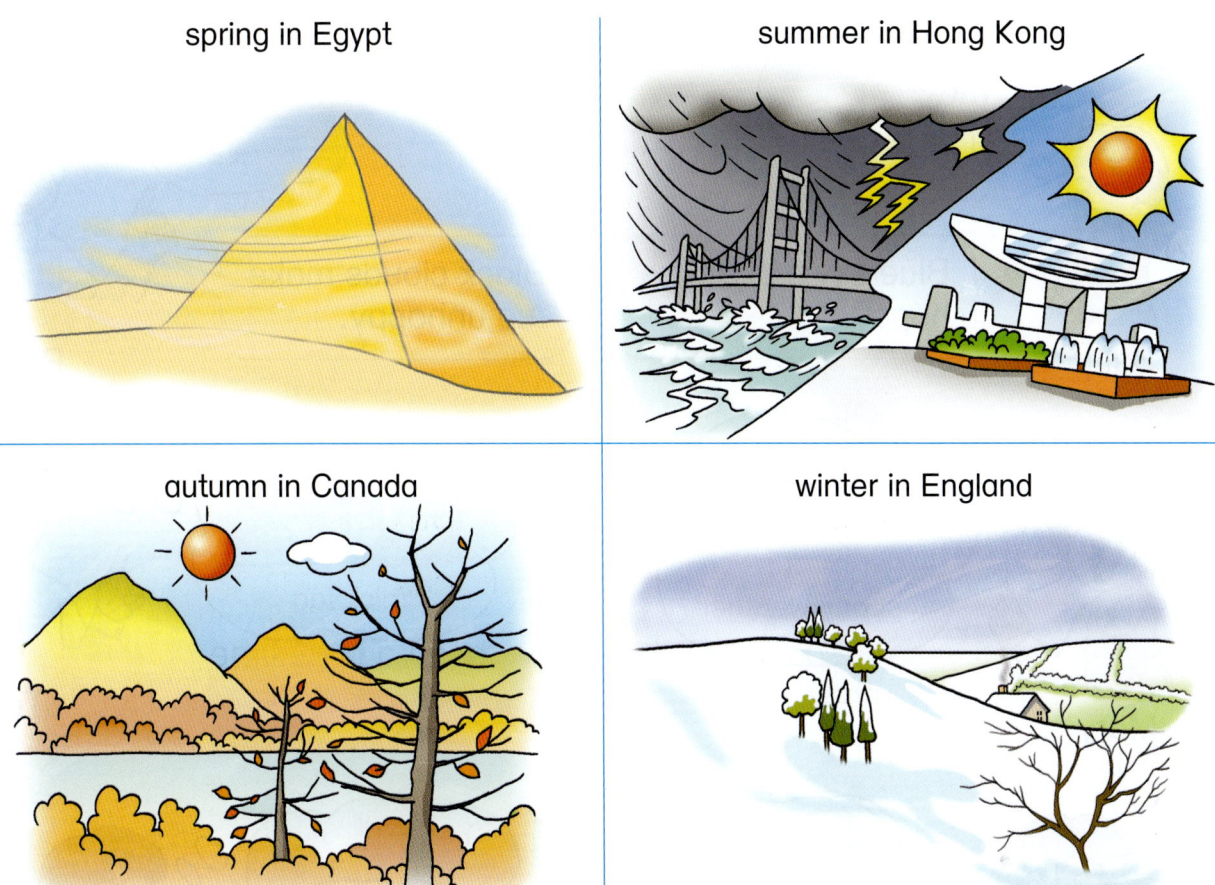

spring in Egypt

summer in Hong Kong

autumn in Canada

winter in England

In spring there are sandstorms in Egypt.
In summer there are fierce storms in Hong Kong

1. loud thunder
2. bright lightning
3. a fierce storm
4. grey sky
5. soft snow
6. thick fog
7. sunny weather

B The children are talking about the weather. Make sentences.

"What weather makes you happy or unhappy, children?"

1. Sally: Blue sky **makes me** happy.
2. Peter: Black clouds **make me unhappy**.
3. Mary — sunny weather
4. Tom — thick fog
5. Candy — loud thunder
6. Charlie — warm sun

Sally likes blue sky.
Peter doesn't like black clouds.

What weather makes you happy or unhappy?

C The children are going to write a poem about the weather. Help them to make the sentences.

1

The sun is hot.
The sun is shining.
➡ The hot sun is shining brightly.

2

The snow is soft.
The snow is falling.
➡ The soft snow is falling lightly.

3

The wind is cool.
The wind is blowing.
➡ The cool wind ...

4

The rain is cold.
The rain is falling.
➡ The cold rain ...

5

The clouds are black.
The clouds are moving.
➡ ...

6

The fog is thick.
The fog is moving.
➡ ...

D **Listen and read. Pinky's winter adventure.**

1 Pinky the polar bear lived in a very cold place. There was snow all year round.

I want to go on holiday. Hong Kong is a good place for my holiday. It's winter there now and the seafood is delicious. Cold weather and seafood make me happy.

2 Pinky bought a ticket to Hong Kong. When she arrived, she was very surprised. Although it was winter, Pinky thought the weather was very warm.

Brr! It's cold here. Where's my coat?

Cold? It's not cold! It's like summer at home.

3 Pinky got in a taxi. By now she was very hot.

Isn't it cold? You're lucky. You've got a nice warm fur coat.

How strange! People here think it's cold but I'm too warm. Is it really winter?

4

I need to find a colder place.

Pinky did not feel well in the hotel. She was hot and hungry.

5 Pinky found the hotel cold store. It was full of food.

Mmm. This seafood is very good. I like Hong Kong now. I think I'll come back again next year!

Where did you last go on holiday? What was the weather like?

E **Are these sentences about the story true or false? Put a ✓ or a ✗.**

1 ☐ Pinky lived in the South Pole.

2 ☐ Pinky thought the weather was cold in Hong Kong so she went to Hong Kong.

3 ☐ The taxi driver thought Pinky was lucky because she had a fur coat.

4 ☐ Pinky went to the hotel swimming pool because she was hot.

5 ☐ Pinky was happy because she found the hotel cold store.

SKILLS Sally wanted to write a poem about summer. First she wrote a list of words about summer.

Summer

blue sky   hot sun shining

Then she wrote the poem.

It's summer, it's summer,
What a lovely season!
Blue sky and hot sun shining,
I like summer.

Now she wants to write another poem. Help her to write a list of words for another season.

F  **Listen. Say this poem.**

AUTUMN

Autumn weather makes me happy.
Cool wind blowing,
Warm sun shining,
And white clouds moving slowly.

Now write a poem about spring. Use some of these words.

Reading. Living in a very cold country.

Jenny and Ayda are pen-friends. Ayda lives in a hot country and Jenny lives in a very cold country. This e-mail is from Jenny to Ayda.

File Edit View Insert Format Tools Compose Help

From: Jenny
Sent: 8th January 2005
To: Ayda
Subject: Winter

Dear Ayda

Thank you for your e-mail and the pictures of your home town.

I'm sending you some pictures of my home town with this e-mail. It's winter now, so there is snow in all the pictures.

Our winter is very different from your winter. Today, it is snowing heavily and the sky is dark. All the trees and houses and fields are white. The wind is blowing, and the temperature is minus 25°C (-25°C). That's colder than the ice-box in the fridge in your kitchen!

There is ice on the river. The ice is so thick that we can walk on it! We can even drive a car on it! The snow is very thick too. The ground floor of my house is often under the snow, so we have a door on the top floor.

Inside, my house is warm and comfortable, but outside we must wear thick clothes. We wear thick socks and gloves to keep our hands warm and a thick hat.

Some people stay inside too much, and that makes them unhealthy and overweight. But I love playing in the snow, and I do winter sports like skating and ice-hockey.

In the summer, the warmer weather comes and makes everyone happy. The snow goes away, and we can see green grass again.

Write again soon.

Jenny

9 Neighbours

A 🎧 **Listen. These people are neighbours. What are they doing?**

Mrs Lee is giving her neighbour a lift.
Jane is lending her neighbour some salt.

1.
give a neighbour a lift

2.
lend a neighbour something

3.
collect a neighbour's post

4.
throw litter

5.
play music loudly

6.
put his belongings in the corridor

B 🎧 Listen and read.

1. Last month Lily moved to a new flat. She came back to the village to see her father. She wanted to talk to him about her new neighbours.

> I'm not very happy in my new home, Father. My neighbours are rude and unhelpful. Why don't they like me?

> Let me tell you a story.

2. One day I was mending my bicycle beside a road **when** a man stopped his car.

> Hey you! Come here. I'm thinking of moving to this village. What are the people like in this neighbourhood?

> Well ... what are the people like in your neighbourhood now?

3. The man complained about his neighbours.

> I don't get on with my neighbours because they're rude. They never say hello. They throw litter out of their windows and they make a lot of noise. They never offer to help me **when** I need it. They're untidy and unkind.

> Well ... I don't think you'll like the people in this neighbourhood either.

What do you think of the man and his neighbours?

4 A few days later I was going home with some boxes when another man stopped his car.

Excuse me, sir. Do you need some help? Would you like a lift?

Yes, please. That's very kind of you.

5 I got in the man's car. We had a chat on the way home.

I'm thinking of moving to this village. Can you tell me what the people are like in this neighbourhood?

Well ... what are the people like in your neighbourhood now?

6 The second man praised his neighbours.

They're very nice. I like them because they're polite and helpful. They take care of my pet when I'm away. We often lend each other things. We often have dinner together.

I think you'll like the people in this neighbourhood too.

7 Thank you for telling me the story, Father. I know now that I must be nice to my neighbours. Then they'll be nice to me.

Yes, you should treat people the way you want them to treat you.

C   Circle the best answers about the story.

1. In picture 2 the man was _____.
   (a) rude   (b) polite   (c) kind

2. The first man was _____ about his neighbours.
   (a) happy   (b) unhappy   (c) worried

3. When the first man needed help, his neighbours _____.
   (a) threw litter out of their windows   (b) made a lot of noise   (c) did not offer to help him

4. The second man helped the old man. He _____.
   (a) lent the old man a car   (b) gave the old man a lift   (c) took care of the old man's pets

5. Her father's story taught Lily how to _____ her neighbours.
   (a) get on with   (b) give lifts to   (c) have dinner with

6. Choose the best title for the story.
   (a) A bad neighbour   (b) Good and bad neighbours   (c) A good neighbour

SKILLS

Read these sentences.

1

The second man was happy.
The first man was unhappy.

2

The second man's neighbours were helpful.
The first man's neighbours were unhelpful.

Match the sentences and the pictures.

1. Tim is untidy.
2. Bobby is unfriendly.
3. Paul is unhappy.

a    b  `1`   c

D 🎧 **Listen and read. Peter and Tom are talking about their neighbours. Make sentences.**

E The children are learning how to be good neighbours. Make sentences.

1	My mother cooks some food for our neighbour	when	(a)	I meet them.
2	I always say hello to my neighbours		(b)	she's away on holiday.
3	I offer to help my neighbour		(c)	she isn't at home.
4	My mother looks after my neighbour's children		(d)	she's sick.
5	I collect my neighbour's post		(e)	she's at home.
			(f)	she needs help.

1 __d__   2 __a__   3 _____   4 _____   5 _____

How do YOU and your family treat your neighbours?

F   Reading. The lion and the mouse.

This is a story about a lion and a mouse who were neighbours. The lion was not a good neighbour. He was often noisy when the mouse wanted to sleep. He was unhelpful and untidy, and he was very unfriendly. He even ate one of the mouse's visitors when he was hungry. The mouse could not complain because the lion was bigger than him.

One day, a man came. The man wanted to catch the lion for a zoo. The man had a very big wooden box. He put a delicious piece of meat in the box and left the box open. Then he went away.

That evening, the lion smelled the meat and followed his nose to the big box. He jumped into the box to get the meat. There was a noise behind him, and the surprised lion was in the dark. The box was closed!

The lion could not open the box from the inside and he could not break it. First, he was angry, then he was afraid. The mouse heard the noise and thought, 'I can't leave my neighbour in there.' So the mouse used his teeth to make a small hole in the box. It was hard work, and the mouse was tired, but he worked all night making the hole bigger. Just before morning, the hole was big enough, and the lion broke out of the box.

After that, the lion was a better neighbour. He was still untidy, but he was less noisy, and he did not eat any more of the mouse's friends.

10 A busy weekend

A  Listen. Mr and Mrs Johnson are on holiday. What is happening at their house?

The robot is doing the housework.
Grandpa is going for a walk.

1.  make a mess
2.  tear the toilet paper
3.  break the vase
4.  do the housework
5.  go for a walk
6.  draw on the wall

VOCABULARY 64

B Mr and Mrs Johnson are worried about Charlie and Cherry. They are checking what they are doing on the computer. What can they see?

1. Charlie **is eating** a sandwich.

He **has eaten** the sandwich.

2. Charlie and Cherry **are drinking** some milk.

They **have drunk** the milk.

3. Charlie is writing an e-mail.

He has _____

4. Cherry is doing her homework.

_____

5. Charlie is drawing a picture.

_____

6. Charlie and Cherry are going out.

_____

Charlie and Cherry are at a cafe. Charlie is checking what the robot has done. Make sentences.

Every day I …	Yesterday I …	I have already …
break	broke	broken
do	did	done
draw	drew	drawn
drink	drank	drunk
eat	ate	eaten
give	gave	given
go	went	gone
swim	swam	swum
take	took	taken
tear	tore	torn
throw	threw	thrown
write	wrote	written

Listen and read. Cherry wrote this poem after talking to her parents on the phone.

Have you been a good girl today?

I've done my homework and I've read my book.
I've eaten my lunch and I've thanked the cook.
I've done the housework and I've played outside.
I've taken my pet for a bicycle ride.
But whatever I've done, they only say...
Have you been a good girl today?

I've been to the zoo and I've seen a monkey.
I've been to the beach and I've swum in the sea.
I've been to the park and I've played on the swing.
I've been to school and I've learned to sing.
But wherever I've been, they only say...
Have you been a good girl today?

E Are these sentences about the poem true or false? Put a ✔ or a ✘.

1. ☐ Cherry did not finish her homework.
2. ☐ She cooked her own lunch.
3. ☐ She went for a walk.
4. ☐ She saw a monkey at the zoo.
5. ☐ She swam in the sea.
6. ☐ She had a piano lesson.

Read the telephone conversation and the message.

 : Hello.

 : Hello, Cherry. It's <u>Mrs Lee</u>. Is your <u>Mother</u> there?

 : No, sorry. She's not here. She's on holiday.

 : OK. Please ask her to <u>call me on</u> 1<u>234</u> 1<u>234</u> when she comes back.

 : OK. Goodbye.

 : Goodbye.

Message for: Mum
From: Mrs Lee
Message: Please call her on 1234 1234.

Work in pairs. Role play the conversation. Then write down the message for Cherry.

Mr Johnson
8989 8989

Mr Taylor

Message for: _____
From: _____
Message: _____

F The pets have made a mess at home. Make sentences.

eat the potato crisps / draw on the wall

break the vase / tear your shirt

drink the milk

eat the plants

Charlie, the pets have made a mess!

The monkey has eaten the potato crisps. It has drawn on the wall. The ...

What have they done?

Please clear up the mess.

Charlie phones the robot half an hour later. What has he done?

swept the floor ✓
cleaned the table
washed the wall ✓

Have you cleared up the mess yet?

I've already swept the floor. I haven't ...

Reading. Robots.

We have seen robots in films like *Star Wars*. These robots are machines that talk and walk like people. They can do a lot of jobs, and they think too. But these robots are only in films. They are not real. So are there any real robots in the world today?

The answer is 'Yes' and 'No'. Nobody has made a robot that can think yet. Nobody has made a robot that can do a lot of different jobs. However, scientists are trying to make them. They have already made some interesting robots.

A Japanese company has made a robot called 'Qrio' (pronounced Cu-ri-o). Qrio can play with you. It can walk and run. It can play with a ball and it can have a conversation. It can also learn your name and remember people's faces.

An American company has made a robot called 'Roomba'. Roomba does not look like a person. Roomba is a robot for cleaning floors. It can clean without any help. Roomba can learn about the furniture in the room, so it does not hit tables and chairs.

Have you seen the Football World Cup on TV? Do you know there is a World Robo Cup too? Every year, teams of robots from many countries meet to play football. There are games for four kinds of robots, small, middle-sized, four-legged and two-legged robots. The robots can't play very well yet, but every year they play better. In the future, will they play better than people? What do you think?

11 Special things we have done

A **Listen. The children are doing some special things at the spring fair. What are they doing?**

Sally is wearing a costume.
Tom is riding a horse.

1.
ride a horse

2.
wear a costume

3.
fly in a balloon

4.
sing on a stage

5.
drive a racing car

6. I've seen a princess.
take a photo of cartoon characters

B Listen and read. The story of Richard Branson.

Meet Sir Richard Branson. He's a famous businessman. Sir Richard has had a very interesting and exciting life so far. Here are some of the special things he has done.

He has started over 100 companies.
Sir Richard started his first company when he was seventeen. Now he runs many different companies. These include travel, music and soft drinks companies. When Sir Richard travels on his own airline, he always helps the staff. He talks to passengers, serves drinks and plays games with children. His airline has won many awards.

He has broken three world records.
Sir Richard enjoys doing dangerous and exciting things. He holds the world records for crossing the Atlantic Ocean by speedboat and balloon. He has also broken the world record for crossing the Pacific Ocean in a balloon.

Sir Richard has twice tried to fly around the world in a balloon. Once there was a fire in his balloon and he had to land in the sea.

Have you ever broken a world record?

Yes, three times.

He has done a lot of work for charity.
Sir Richard does not like smoking or cigarette advertising. So he started a charity called 'Parents Against Tobacco'. He also gives a lot of money to other charities.

He has bought an island.
Sir Richard spends his holidays on his own island. He always invites some of his staff to join him. He enjoys talking to them and listening to their ideas. Drivers, watchmen, air hostesses, pilots and secretaries have all had holidays on Sir Richard's island.

He has written hundreds of letters to his staff.
Sir Richard is one of the richest businessmen in the world but he still cares a lot about people. He writes his staff a letter every month and has a big party for them every year. They can write to him whenever they like and he always replies. 'If my staff are happy, then my customers will be happy too,' he says.

C Answer the questions.

1 What does Sir Richard do when he travels on his own airline?
2 Has Sir Richard ever broken a world record?
3 What world records has he broken?
4 Has he ever flown in a balloon?
5 Has he given money to charity?
6 Who does he invite to join him on holiday?
7 Do you think Sir Richard is a good boss? Why?

 Read the first section of the passage again.

First section

Main idea: Sir Richard's companies
Details: 1 He started his first business at seventeen.
2 He has started different types of companies.
3 His airline is very famous.

Now read the second and fourth sections of the passage again. One of the details listed below does not fit the main idea in the section. Underline it.

Second section

Main idea: Sir Richard's world records
Details: 1 He has crossed the Atlantic Ocean by boat.
2 He has crossed the Atlantic Ocean by balloon.
3 He likes travelling to different countries.
4 He has crossed the Pacific Ocean by balloon.

Fourth section

Main idea: Sir Richard's island
Details: 1 He has an island.
2 He likes to spend his holidays with his staff.
3 His island is very big.
4 He likes talking to his staff.

D The teacher is asking the children about the special things they have done. Make sentences.

Composition: Special things I have done

Have you ever done anything special, children?

1. speak – spoken

Candy: I've spoken to a famous person.

2. see – seen

Sally: I've seen a princess.

3. ride – ridden

Peter: I've ridden a camel.

4. sing – sung

Mary: I've sung in a concert.

5. fly – flown

Tom: fly a helicopter

6. wear – worn

Charlie: wear a costume

7. take – taken

Betty: take a photo of a cartoon character

8. write – written

Tina: write a letter to my uncle

E Now the children are doing a survey about special things they have done.

	How many times have you...?	Mary	Tom	You	Your friend
1	worn a costume	✓✓✓	✓✓		
2	driven a racing car	✗	✓		
3	spoken to a film star	✓	✗		
4	ridden a horse	✓	✓✓		
5	seen a famous person	✓	✗		
6	been to other countries	✓✓	✓✓✓		
7	taken a photo of cartoon characters	✓✓✓	✓		

✓ = once   ✓✓ = twice   ✓✓✓ = three times   ✗ = never

1 I've worn a costume three times. Have you ever worn a costume?

Yes, I've worn a costume twice.

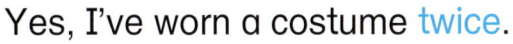

2 I've never driven a racing car. Have you ever driven a racing car?

Yes, I've driven a racing car once.

3 I've spoken to a film star once. Have you ever spoken to a film star?

No, I've never spoken to a film star.

Now tick the grid and ask your friend.

F Reading. Amazing record breakers.

Metwali Mathna from Egypt and Tsuchida Wakado from Japan are both famous athletes. Mathna is a weight lifter. He has broken world records for weight lifting many times. Wakado holds the world record for the women's marathon. But that is not the only thing that makes them special. Both Mathna and Wakado are disabled - they cannot use their legs.

Tsuchida Wakado races in a wheelchair because she can't run. The fastest male runner can run a marathon in 2 hours and 4 minutes. But Wakado, in her wheelchair, has done it in 1 hour and 32 minutes!

Metwali Mathna lost the use of his legs when he was a boy. He started weight lifting as a hobby and found that he was good at it. Now he can lift more than able-bodied lifters, and he has won two gold medals at the Paralympic Games.

The biggest sporting event in the world is the Olympic Games. Every four years, athletes from all over the world come together and try to break world records. The Paralympic Games are the second biggest sporting event. Nearly 4,000 disabled athletes from more than 130 countries come to these Games. More than 800,000 people watch them, and more than 1,000,000,000 people watch on TV.

The best athletes win gold medals. The second best win silver medals and the third best win bronze medals. One disabled athlete has won 54 medals! Her name is Tricia Zorn. She is a swimmer from the USA and she can't see. She has won more medals than any other athlete in the world.

12 Trees

A Listen. Talk about the trees in the picture.

1. broad leaves
2. long branches
3. short branches
4. narrow leaves
5. thick trunk
6. thin trunk
7. shallow roots
8. deep roots

This tree has a thick trunk. That tree has a thin trunk.

VOCABULARY 78

B Tina is writing about her favourite tree. Help Tina to finish her writing. Use some of these words to help you.

long   broad   thick

us   me   them   it   her   him

There is a tree outside my window. It has _____ leaves and _____ branches. It is fifty years old and has a very _____ trunk. The tree is very useful. It keeps me cool. Jane swings in the tree. The tree gives her lots of fun. Dad reads books under it. It gives _____ shade. Animals live in the tree. The tree gives _____ food. The tree has been our good friend. We love _____ and it loves _____.

shade

D Listen to the poem.

Trees

There's a tree outside my window,
Whose branches keep me cool.
There's a tree whose branches beckon,
While on my way to school.

There's a tree upon the hillside,
Whose roots run long and deep.
There's a tree beside a river,
Whose branches bend and weep.

There's a tree up on the hilltop,
In which the songbirds nest.
There's a tree deep in the jungle,
In which the monkeys rest.

There's a tree beside the desert,
Whose branches provide shade.
There's a tree beside the seaside,
In which a home is made.

by Mike Murphy

Is there a special tree in your neighbourhood? Tell the class about it.

E Answer the questions.

1 Where is the tree that keeps the poet cool?
2 Which tree has deep roots?
3 Where is the tree whose branches bend and weep?
4 What do birds make in trees?
5 Where do monkeys live?
6 Which part of a tree gives us shade?
7 Where do the songbirds nest?
8 What is beside the seaside?

 Read these sentences.

> This is the main idea of the paragraph.
>
> Trees are important to people. They give us shade. They make the air clean.

Now read some more facts about trees. Choose one or two to finish the above paragraph. Write sentences.

take in / sunlight and rain
keep / cool
make / cities green and healthy
have / deep roots

F The children are in the country park. Ask and answer questions about trees.

Why are trees important?

They hold the soil together.
They give us food and wood.
Birds and animals live in them.
They are beautiful.
They make cities green and healthy.
They make the air clean.
They give us shade.
They make cities less noisy.

Why are trees useful?

Trees are useful because they hold the soil together.

Why must we look after trees?

We must look after trees because birds and animals live in them.

Why do we need trees?

We need trees because they make the air clean.

PRACTICE

Reading. The most useful tree in the world.

Some trees give us fruit to eat, like, apple trees and orange trees. Other trees provide wood for furniture and houses. A few trees can grow without much water. But only one kind of tree can do all these things – the palm tree.

There are 2,500 different kinds of palm trees, and the most useful kinds are date palms. Good date palms provide 400 kilos of dates every year for 70 years. Dates are delicious and healthy, and you can keep them longer than other fruit. Apples and oranges are not good after a week in hot weather, but dates are good for many weeks.

Every part of a palm tree is useful. The leaves and branches provide cool shade. They are important for people and animals in hot countries. In cold weather, the dry leaves and branches can make fires to keep people warm. People make baskets and other things from the leaves. They can make houses from the branches and long thick trunks.

Palm trees can grow in very dry countries because they do not need much water. They need water only once every two weeks. They do not need good soil either. They can grow in sandy soil, and they help to stop the sand moving.

Palm trees are beautiful too. Their tall trunks and green leaves provide colour and interest. People in deserts and hot dry cities have loved palm trees for hundreds of years.

13 Eating habits

A 🎧 Listen. The children are in a restaurant. What do they have on their trays?

Harry has meat and fries. He has a soft drink.
Tom has fish and rice. He also has tea.

1. healthy
2. unhealthy
3. vegetables
4. soft drinks
5. meat
6. fresh fruit
7. fried food
8. fish

B The school nurse is telling the children about a healthy diet. Make sentences.

This is Fred. He has an unhealthy diet.
He eats too much meat.
He drinks too many soft drinks.
He doesn't eat enough vegetables.
He ...

C Harry is having lunch with Tom. Read their conversation.

"You look fit, Tom. How can I get fit like you?"

"I have a healthy diet.
1. I eat plenty of vegetables and fruit.
2. I don't eat too many sweets.
3. I don't eat too much fried food.
4. I don't drink too many soft drinks.
5. I drink plenty of water."

Tom is giving Harry some friendly advice. Finish the sentences.

1. Eat plenty of vegetables and fruit.
2. Don't eat too many sweets.
3. _____
4. _____
5. _____

D   **Listen and read. Harry goes to Fit Camp.**

Harry was overweight. He was unhappy because he could not run as fast as the other children.

'What's the matter, Harry?' his mother asked. 'I'm too fat. I can't keep up with the others,' said Harry. 'Have a look at this newspaper article. I've just read about a camp for children like you,' said his mother.

Getting Fit at Fit Camp

Dr Alfred has started a camp to help overweight children get fit. 'Many children round the world are overweight because they eat too much fried food and too many sweets. Fried food and sweets are not good for them,' says Dr Alfred. Children can go to this camp in the holidays. They learn to eat healthy food and take exercise.

Harry went to Fit Camp in the summer holidays. His mother went too. Harry learned to choose food that was good for him. He found that healthy food tasted nice. His mother learned how to cook healthy food for her family. Every day Harry did some exercise. He made friends with the other children at the camp. He was much happier.

When Harry went back to school, he was healthy and fit. The other children were very surprised when they saw him. 'Wow! What happened to you, Harry?' they said. Harry laughed happily. 'I've been to a great camp and I've learned to eat healthy food,' he said. After that, Harry could join in all the games at school.

E **Are these sentences about the story true or false? Put a ✔ or a ✘.**

1. ☐ Harry was unhappy because he ate too much.
2. ☐ His mother read about Fit Camp in the newspaper.
3. ☐ Dr Alfred started Fit Camp to help children to get fat.
4. ☐ Harry's mother learned about healthy food at Fit Camp.
5. ☐ Harry was surprised when he went back to school.

Harry is watching a TV programme about healthy old people. Read about Granny Kate's eating habits.

You're very healthy, Granny Kate. What advice can you give us about a healthy diet?

Don't eat too much salted food. Salted food is not good for us.
Eat plenty of vegetables and fruit. Vegetables and fruit are good for us.
Don't drink too much coffee. Coffee is not good for us.
Don't eat too many sweets. Sweets are not good for us.
Drink plenty of water. Water is good for us.

Harry's grandmother is asking him about Granny Kate. Make sentences.

Why is Granny Kate so healthy?

Because she has a healthy diet.
She doesn't eat too much salted food.
She eats plenty of vegetables and fruit. She …

Reading. Ten ways to good health.

1. **Eat Breakfast!**
Breakfast is the most important meal of the day. After a long night without food, you need a big breakfast. Children who eat breakfast do better at school.

2. **Move!**
Don't always go by car or by bus. Walk, run or ride a bicycle. Don't go up in a lift. Walk up the stairs. When you watch TV or use a computer, get up and move sometimes.

3. **Snacks and sweets are OK!**
BUT... don't eat too many! Too much sugar is bad for you. Try eating apples instead of sweets.

4. **Make your heart strong!**
Run, swim or play sport three times a week. Less than that is not enough. Start slowly and then go faster. This will make your heart stronger.

5. **Eat different things!**
Don't eat too much of one thing. For example, meat is good for you, but too much meat is bad for you. Try to eat lots of different things.

6. **Go out with friends!**
With your friends, don't just play computer games. Play real games. Walk, swim, cycle, run or play sports with friends.

7. **Eat vegetables!**
OK. You don't like vegetables, but they are very important. Eat three vegetables and two pieces of fruit every day.

8. **Join in sports at school!**
It's a good way to feel good, look good and keep fit.

9. **Don't get too much or too little sun!**
Too much sun on your skin is very bad for you. But no sun is very bad too.

10. **Try new things!**
Try new sports and games and new kinds of food. Don't be afraid. You will find new ways to enjoy keeping healthy.

14 A healthy meal

A 🎧 Listen. The children are having a buffet lunch. What food do they like?

Candy likes fruit cakes and grapes.
Sam likes steamed fish and fried rice.

1. fruit cakes
2. soup
3. prawns
4. roast beef
5. steamed fish
6. fried rice
7. chicken wings
8. grapes

B Peter and Sally have taken a lot of food. Talk about the food on their plates.

There is a lot of fish on Sally's plate. There are a few prawns and a lot of vegetables.
There is a little fish on Peter's plate. There are a lot of prawns and a few vegetables.

There is	a little / a lot of	meat	bread	fruit
		rice	cheese	soup
		fish	ice cream	juice
There are	a few / a lot of	grapes	potatoes	chicken wings
		prawns	vegetables	fruit cakes

C Who has more food, Peter or Sally? Tick the grid. Tell your friend.

	Peter			Sally		
	a lot of	a little	a few	a lot of	a little	a few
prawns	✓					✓
chicken wings	✓					✓
fish		✓		✓		
soup		✓		✓		
vegetables						
fruit cakes						

Peter has more prawns than Sally.
Sally has fewer chicken wings than Peter.
Sally has more fish than Peter.
Peter has less soup than Sally.

Whose meal do you think is healthier?

Now talk about Sam and Candy's food.

LANGUAGE FOCUS 94

D Listen and read.

1

The Big family loved eating sweets and fried food. 'We're all too fat. We must go on a diet. We should eat less food and exercise more,' said Mrs Big.

2

One day Mrs Big's sister came to visit them. She gave the family a chocolate cake. 'Oh, look! It's a cake! Shall we eat it now or later?' said Mr Big.
'We won't eat it now. We'll keep it for visitors. Cake is not good for us. We're on a diet. Remember?' said Mrs Big.

3

That night Mr Big could not sleep. He went to the kitchen.
Mr Big said, 'Chocolate cake is my favourite. I'll just cut a small piece.'
Mr Big ate some cake and went back to bed.

After a while, Billy went to the kitchen. Billy said, 'We only had salad for dinner. I'm so hungry. I must eat something. I know! I'll have a piece of that cake.' Billy ate some cake and went back to bed.

4

Mrs Big couldn't sleep either. 'I can't stop thinking about that cake in the kitchen. I can't wait any longer. I must have a piece.' said Mrs Big.

Mrs Big went to the kitchen. 'Why is there only one piece left?' she asked.

5

Mr Big and Billy heard the noise in the kitchen. They went in and turned on the light. 'Aha! We've caught you! You said we mustn't eat the cake. So what are you doing?' said Mr Big.
'Well,... all elephants are big. We shouldn't go on a diet,' she said.

The Big family were very happy. No more diets!

Now act the story.

E   Answer the questions. Give short answers.

1   Mrs Big said her family could not eat the cake. Why?
2   Find words that mean 'eating less to get thin'.
3   Where did the Big family keep the cake?
4   Why were they hungry?
5   Who had the first piece of cake?
6   Circle the best title for the play?
     (a) Mrs Big's cake   (b) The thin elephants   (c) The Big family's diet

F Charlie and Cherry are talking about what to have for lunch. Make sentences.

I want Set A.
There's a lot of meat. There are a few vegetables too.
There's a little rice.
There's a lot of ice cream. There are a few grapes too.

I want Set B.
There's …

Whose meal is healthier? Why?

_____ has less meat than _____.

He/She has _____ vegetables than _____.

_____

_____

_____

I think _____'s meal is healthier.

Reading. The old man at the party.

One day, an old man went to a party in a big house. There was a lot of food and drink, and there were a lot of people. Most of the people were in expensive clothes, but the old man was in old clothes. When he arrived, a servant told him to sit at a table for poor people. The people in good clothes were at different tables.

The servants brought food to the people in good clothes first. Then they brought food to the poor people. But the poor people got less food. Then the servants brought more food: meat, rice, green vegetables and potatoes. The poor people got less rice and meat and fewer vegetables than the others. After that, there were fruit cakes, but the old man and the poor people did not get any of them.

The old man was still hungry. So he got up and went home. He put on good clothes, new shoes, and his most expensive jacket. Then he came back to the party.

A servant was standing at the door of the big house. The servant saw the old man's good clothes and welcomed him politely and took him to the best table. All the most important people were at this table, and there was a lot of food and delicious drinks. The old man sat down and ate and drank. Then he took off his jacket and put it in the food.

'Why are you putting your jacket in your food?' the other people asked. The old man answered, 'In this house, they think my clothes are more important than me. So my clothes must eat more than me!'

15 Places we visit

A  Listen. Where can the Johnson family go at the weekend? What can they do?

Exciting Places To Visit In London

The London Eye
– look down on London

London Zoo
– watch animals

The New Wembley Stadium
– watch a football match

The National Gallery
– see famous paintings

Covent Garden
– see the clowns

A toyshop
– buy a big teddy bear

They can visit the London Eye and look down on London.
They can visit the National Gallery and see famous paintings.

B It is Saturday afternoon. Mr Johnson is taking Charlie to a football match. Mrs Johnson is taking Cherry to Covent Garden. Make sentences.

Mr Johnson:	We can go to the New Wembley Stadium by bus or by the underground.
Charlie:	How long does it take to get there on the underground?
Mr Johnson:	It takes about thirty minutes.
Charlie:	How long ...?
Mr Johnson:	It ...
Charlie:	Let's take the ... then.

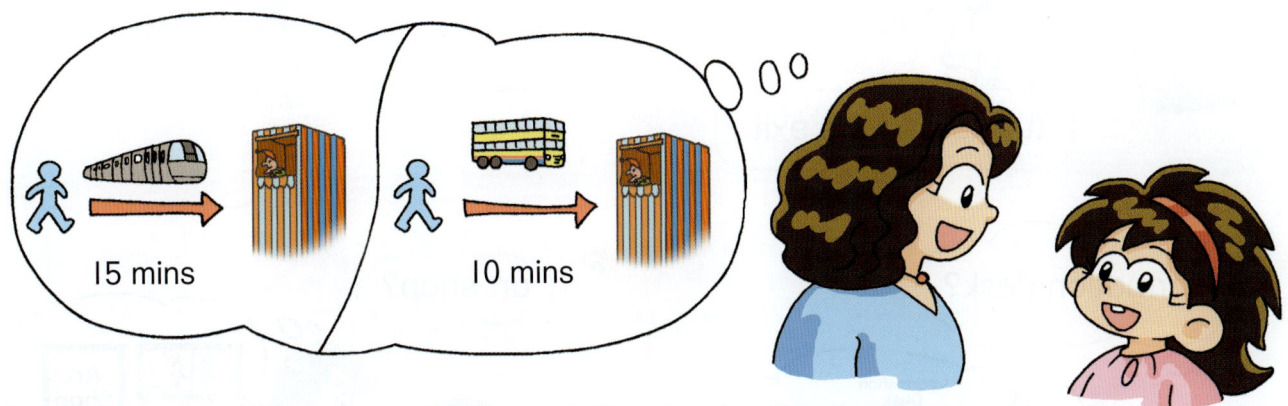

Mrs Johnson:	We can go to Covent Garden by the underground or bus.
Cherry:	How long...?
	:
	:
Cherry:	Let's ...

LANGUAGE FOCUS 100

C   Mrs Johnson and Cherry are at the National Gallery. Make sentences.

next to   behind   between

1 Excuse me. Where are the toilets?

They're *behind* the cloakroom.

2 Excuse me. Where's the art library?

It's *between* the gallery and the restaurant.

3 Excuse me. Where's the escalator?

It's *next to* the exit.

4 coffee shop?

5 information desk?

6 art shop?

101   LANGUAGE FOCUS

D **Listen and read. Billy and the monster.**

1

Tomorrow we'll go on a field trip to the marshes. A marsh is a very wet place. Sometimes there's a lot of mist. The marshes are famous because a lot of rare birds live there.

'How long does it take to get from here to the marsh?' one of the children asked the teacher. 'It takes an hour by bus,' she replied. 'Now remember. You must stay together and follow me.'

2

Why did the teacher tell us to stay together?

Because there's a monster in the marsh. It chases children.

Billy was not a nice boy. He liked to frighten the other children. He told his classmates stories about a monster in the marsh.

3

On the day of the field trip, the children walked behind the teacher. Billy walked slowly at the back of the line. The mist got thicker and it started to rain. Soon Billy could not see the others.

4

Suddenly there was a loud noise. A white shape flew over Billy's head. He thought it was a marsh monster.

5

Billy screamed and ran to the teacher. The children and the teacher stopped. They laughed when they saw a white bird flying out of the mist.

Have you ever been on a field trip? Do you remember what happened? Tell your friend.

E Answer the questions. Circle the best answers about the story.

1   Find a word that means 'something we do not see very often.'

2   Which picture shows 'mist'? Circle the correct picture.
    (a)    (b)    (c)

3   How did Billy frighten the other children?

    He told them about _____ at the marshes.

4   Why couldn't Billy see the others? Give two reasons.

5   What made Billy think there was a monster? Say two things.

F On Sunday, the Johnson family go to a fair. Ask and answer questions about the shops.

Excuse me. Where's the Clown Corner, please?

It's behind the Doll Shop.

1 Clown Corner (5 mins)
2 Popcorn Shop (4 mins)
3 Goldfish Catch (4 mins)
4 Drinks Shop (5 mins)
5 Pancake Shop (4 mins)

How long does it take to walk there?

About five minutes.

Thank you very much.

Reading. Visiting the Great Pyramid.

The Great Pyramid in Egypt is one of the biggest buildings in the world. Most buildings last a few hundred years or less, but the Great Pyramid has been there more than 4,500 years. The Egyptians built it for their king, and it took more than twenty years to build. When the king died, they put him in a room inside the Pyramid.

You can visit the Great Pyramid if you go to Cairo, the capital of Egypt. The Great Pyramid is at Giza, a few kilometres from Cairo. A taxi or a bus from Cairo to Giza takes about 20 minutes. The best time to go is early in the morning. After that, there are too many people, and it gets hot.

When you stand near the Great Pyramid, you feel very small! It takes 10 or 15 minutes to walk around it. Some people ride around it on a horse or a camel.

The King's room is in the middle of the Pyramid. You must walk down a long narrow passage under the Pyramid. Some people don't like this and they feel afraid. For most people, it is strange and exciting to be in the room where the king was 4,500 years ago.

There is another way to see inside the Great Pyramid. You can use the Internet. There are hundreds of pictures of the Great Pyramid on the Internet and there is lots of interesting information.

An Internet tour is quicker than a real tour. It takes only a few minutes. But the real Pyramid is much more exciting than a picture can be.

16 Our favourite TV programmes

A Listen. What are the people watching?

Mr Mo is watching a nature programme.
Sally is watching a drama.

1. the news
2. the weather report
3. a cartoon
4. a nature programme
5. a quiz show
6. a drama
7. a cookery programme

B Sally and her family are filling in a questionnaire about the programmes people like to watch. Make sentences.

A survey on favourite TV programmes in a family

1 Which programmes do your family like best?

	M/F	Age	news and weather reports	cartoons	nature programmes	quiz shows	sports programmes	dramas	Reasons
①	M	36	✓						
②	F	34			✓				
③	F	10						✓	
④	M	7		✓					
⑤	F	68				✓			
⑥	M	70					✓		

Why do you like watching nature programmes?

Because they're interesting.

Why do you like watching cartoons?

Because they're amusing.

Which programmes do YOUR family like best? Why?

107 LANGUAGE FOCUS

C One month later, Sally and her family receive the results of the survey. Sally's father is looking at the results. Make sentences.

> Remember the survey we did, children? Well, here are the results.
> Elderly people like watching quiz shows more than news and weather reports.
> Men like watching news and weather reports more than nature programmes.

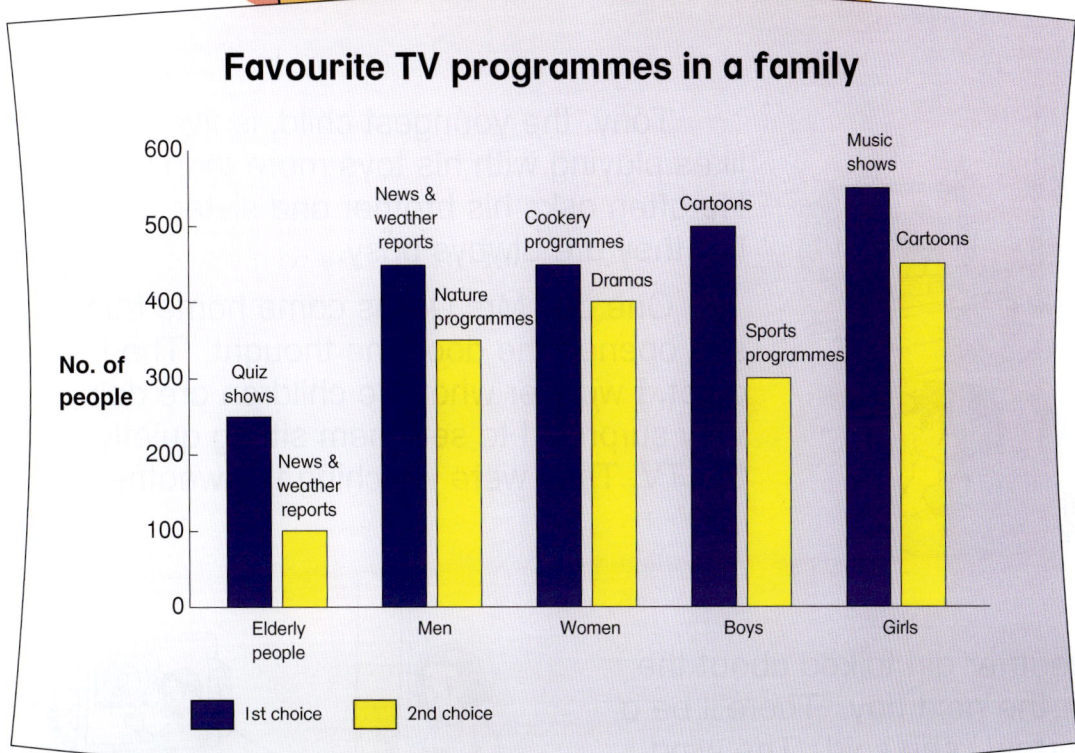

Which of these programmes do you like more? Tell your friend.

1. music shows/quiz shows
2. news and weather reports/nature programmes
3. dramas/cartoons
4. sports programmes/cookery programmes

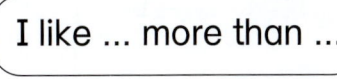

I like ... more than ...

D Listen and read. Tony's happy day.

The Dallas family have three children. Eric and Nancy like watching TV. Eric likes cartoons and Nancy likes music shows. If the programmes are on at the same time, the children sometimes argue about which one to watch.

Tony, the youngest child, is five years old. He likes playing with his toys more than watching TV. He often asks his brother and sister to play with him but they are always busy.

One day Mrs Dallas came home from work. As she opened the door she thought, 'The flat is very quiet. I wonder what the children are doing.' She was very surprised to see them sitting quietly in front of the TV. They were watching the weather report!

The weather girl talked about the weather for the next day. 'There'll be a storm tomorrow,' she said. 'The wind will be strong and there'll be a lot of rain.' 'Oh no!' said Eric and Nancy. They looked upset.

'What's wrong, children?' asked Mrs Dallas. 'I can't have a barbecue in the park tomorrow,' said Eric. 'And I can't go to the beach with my friends,' said Nancy sadly.

Mrs Dallas looked at Tony. He was very happy. 'Great! Everyone will stay at home and play with me. We can play hide-and-seek and have great fun!' he said excitedly.

E Answer the questions about the story.

1. What kind of TV programmes do Eric and Nancy like watching?
2. Why do the children sometimes argue about their favourite TV programmes?
3. Why don't Eric and Nancy play with Tony?
4. Why was Mrs Dallas surprised when she came home from work?
5. What programme were the children watching?
6. What did the weather girl say about the weather for the next day?
7. Why were Eric and Nancy upset after watching the weather report?

Skills Look at the TV guide. Answer the questions.

Channel 1	Channel 2
2:30 Drama: The Big family	2:45 Cookery: Enjoy cooking
3:30 Nature: Insects	3:15 Cartoon: Jojo's journey
4:20 Sport: Golf	3:45 Pop music: Top 10

1. What is on Channel 1 at 2:30? Drama: The Big family.
2. When can you watch a cartoon on Channel 2?
3. What is on Channel 2 at 3:45?
4. What is after the nature programme on Channel 1?

F. The children have finished their homework. They are talking about what programmes to watch.

Channel 1		Channel 2	
5:30	Cartoon: My pet Didi	5:40	Sport: English soccer
6:30	News & the weather report	6:30	Nature: All about lions
7:00	Drama: The Joy family	7:15	Quiz show
8:00	Film: Space travel	8:00	Pop music: Sing! Sing! Sing!

Bobby: Let's watch the cartoon. I like watching cartoons more than sports programmes.
Tom: Why?
Bobby: Because cartoons are amusing.
Tom: But I like watching sports programmes more than cartoons.
Bobby: Why?
Tom: Because sports programmes are exciting.
Lily: Yes, I like sports programmes too.
Bobby: OK. Let's watch the sports programmes at 5:40 then.

It is 6:30 now. The children are talking about what to watch next. Complete the sentences.

Lily: Let's watch the _____. I like _____.

Bobby: Why?

Lily: Because _____.

Bobby: But I like _____.

Lily: Why?

Bobby: _____.

Tom: _____.

Lily: _____.

Reading. No TV.

This is a true story. It happened a few years ago in a small town.

All the families in the town watched a lot of TV, but many people were not happy about this. Some people said, 'TV is bad for us. It makes us lazy and unhealthy.' Others said, 'TV is bad for children because there is too much fighting on TV.' Many people said, 'People don't talk when the TV is on, and that's bad for families.'

One person said, 'Let's stop watching TV - just for one month.' A lot of people liked that idea. So 40 families put their TVs in a cupboard and did not watch TV for one month.

Those four weeks, with no TV, were very different. Children played together more than before. Families talked together more and did interesting things together. One father said, 'When we had TV, we did not talk much, but now we enjoy talking and laughing together. That's more interesting and more amusing than TV.' A boy said, 'I've started new hobbies, and I've had a lot of fun with my brother and parents.'

Some fat children lost a few kilos because they spent less time sitting down. They felt fitter and looked better. Others had more time for homework and did better at school. Nearly everybody enjoyed the month with no TV.

So what happened at the end of the month? Did the 40 families throw their TVs away or did they put the TVs back in their living rooms? The answer is surprising. Not one family threw out their TV! Some people watched less than before, but none of them stopped. They all loved that box in the living room too much!

17 Pocket money

A Listen. How do the children spend their pocket money?

Charlie spends his money on comics and CDs.
Peter spends his money on snacks and drinks.

1. models
2. stationery
3. CDs
4. magazines
5. clothes
6. spend
7. save

B The children are talking about their favourite things. Make sentences.

C. The children are doing a survey on how they spend their pocket money. Make sentences.

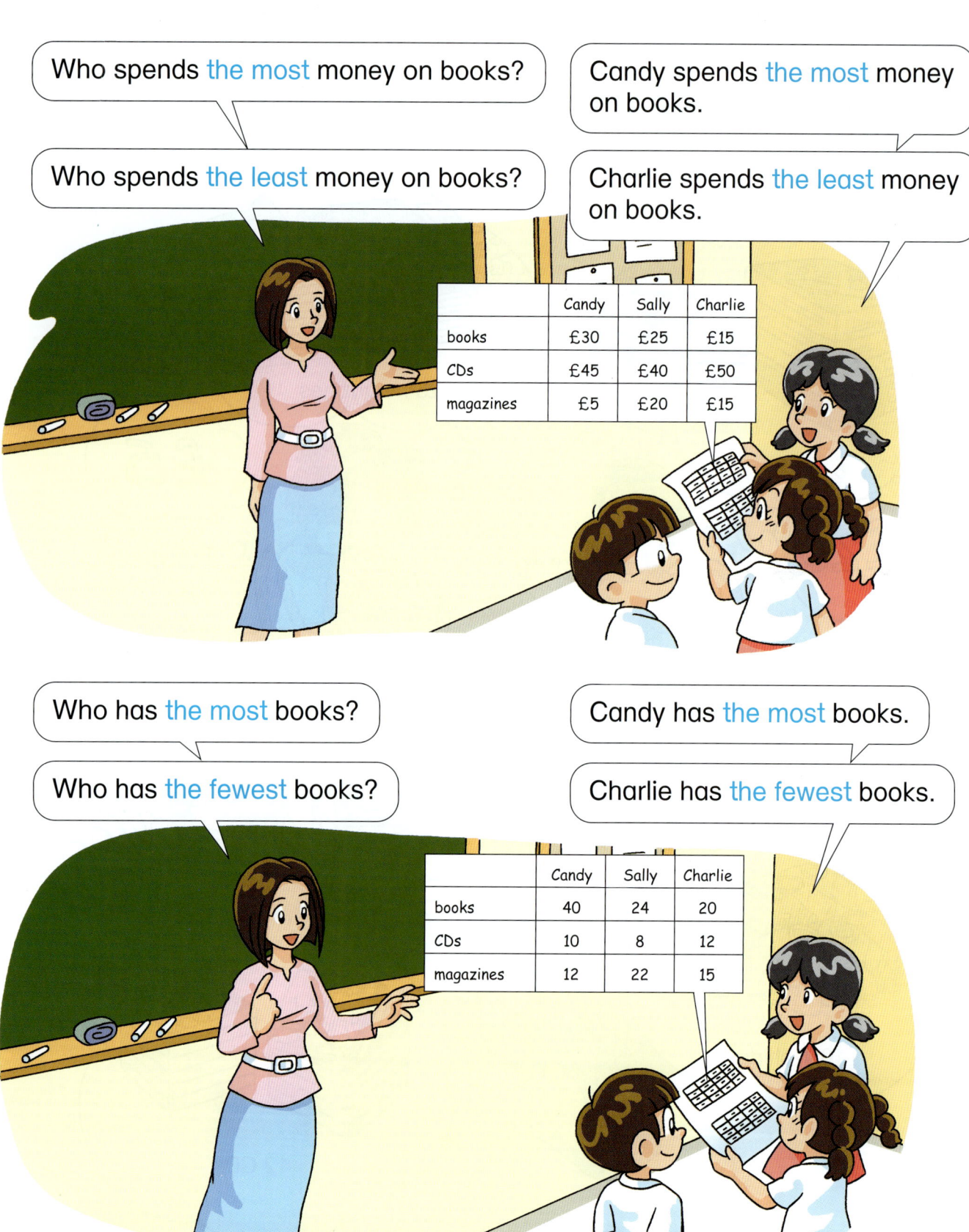

D   **Listen and read. Joyce's pocket money.**

Joyce, Tessa and Tina are sisters. Tina is the eldest. She gets the most pocket money but she spends the least. Joyce is the youngest. She gets the least pocket money but she spends the most. She spends all her money on toys.

One Saturday Joyce was going to meet Tessa and Tina at the shopping centre. Joyce's mother took out her purse. 'Here's your pocket money,' she said. 'And take this money to your sisters: £10 for you, £15 for Tessa and £20 for Tina.'

Before going to the shopping centre, Joyce stopped at a shop. She wanted to buy a birthday present for Tina. 'How much are the hair clips?' she asked. 'They're £1 each. How many do you want?' said the salesman. 'I want these four, please,' said Joyce.

As Joyce took a £10 note out of her purse, a strong wind blew it out of her hand. She ran after it as fast as she could. But the note blew away and she could not get it back.

'Sorry I'm late. Here's your pocket money,' said Joyce when she met her sisters. 'What's wrong, Joyce? Why are you looking so sad?' asked Tessa. 'My pocket money blew away. Now I can't buy a birthday present for Tina,' said Joyce.

'Don't worry. It was my £10 note that blew away, not yours. Now take this money and buy the present,' said Tessa. 'And take this to buy a toy,' said Tina. Joyce was very happy. Now she had the most pocket money!

E Answer the questions about the story. Give short answers.

1. Who saves the most pocket money?
2. How much pocket money does Joyce get?
3. What does Joyce spend her pocket money on?
4. What did Joyce want to buy Tina for her birthday?
5. Why couldn't Joyce buy the present?
6. How much pocket money did Joyce have in the end?
7. Which sister do you like best? Why?

F   Mr and Mrs Lee want their children to write down how they spend their pocket money. Act the children.

Mr and Mrs Lee are looking at the children's table. Make sentences.

	Bobby	Tom	Lily
Pocket money (a month)	£12	£15	£20
Saves	£1	£4	£3
Spends on:			
• toys	£2	£4	£1
• books & magazines	£2	£2	£4
• clothes	£2	£3	£8
• stationery	£1	£1	£2
• snacks	£4	£1	£2

Now do a survey on how you and your friends spend your pocket money.

Reading. Pocket money in Britain.

Most children between 10 and 16 in Britain get some pocket money every week or every month. Most of them get it from their parents, but a few get it from grandparents.

Some children save some of the money, but most of them spend it quickly on extra clothes, going out, music, mobile phones, computer games, magazines, sweets, drinks and snacks. Boys buy the most sweets, drinks and snacks. Girls spend the most on clothes, presents and going out with friends.

I get pocket money every week. I must be good or my mum stops my money. I've got a lot of friends, so I spend a lot on my mobile phone. And I love chocolate!
Gareth, 12

I don't get pocket money every week or every month. My parents give me money when I need it. I spend most of it on my phone and going out with friends.
Helen, 12

I've got a lot of brothers and sisters, and I'm the youngest, so I get the least pocket money. I use most of it to buy clothes and presents for my friends and family.
Jenny, 10

I get some money from my grandparents and from my dad. I save some of it, but I spend most of it on snacks and going out with friends.
Iain, 11

My parents give me money every month. I try not to spend it all at the beginning of the month! I save some of it to buy computer games, and I spend some on sweets.
James, 11

I don't get any pocket money, but I don't mind because I don't like sweets very much. People give me money on my birthday and other special days. I save most of it.
Victoria, 11

18 Our hobbies

A 🎧 **Listen. The children are at the Youth Centre. What are their hobbies?**

Mary's hobby is doing ballet.

1  do ballet	2  play the violin	3  make models	4 collect coins
5  surf the Internet	6  paint pictures	7  make handicrafts	8  grow flowers

VOCABULARY 120

B There is a Collector's Club at the Youth Centre. Peter is the chairman of the club. He is doing a survey of things the children collect. Make sentences.

Welcome to the Collector's Club!		
Name	Collects	First collected
Peter	coins	1999
Betty	dolls	1998
Sally	dolls	1998
Charlie	stamps	2001
Cherry	stamps	2001
Sam	stickers	2000
Tom	model cars	1997

I've collected coins since 1999.
Betty and Sally have collected dolls since 1998.

| 1998 | nineteen ninety-eight | 1999 | nineteen ninety-nine |
| 2000 | two thousand | 2001 | two thousand and one |

LANGUAGE FOCUS

D **Listen and read. Albert gets a reward.**

Albert likes collecting stamps. He has collected stamps for five years. One day he went to the post office to buy some new stamps.

On the way, Albert saw an old man sitting by the road. 'Are you all right?' Albert asked him. 'I've fallen over,' said the old man.

Albert called an ambulance. Then he sat down next to the old man. 'My name's Albert,' he said. 'I'm going to the post office to buy some new stamps for my collection.' 'Oh! You're a stamp collector. How long have you collected stamps?' asked the old man. 'Since 1996,' said Albert.

The ambulance arrived. 'Thank you very much,' said the old man. 'I'm afraid it'll be too late for you to buy the new stamps now.' 'Never mind, sir,' said Albert. 'I hope you'll get better soon.'

Will Albert get the new stamps?

Albert rushed to the post office but he was too late. The new stamps were sold out.

A week later, Albert received a letter from the old man. Inside was a stamp. The old man wrote: 'Thank you for helping me. You are a very kind and unselfish boy. Please take this stamp for your collection. It is very old and valuable.'

Have you ever helped anyone? What did you do?

E   **Answer the questions about the story.**

1. What was the matter with the old man? Circle the correct answer.

    (a) He was poor.   (b) He could not walk.   (c) He was sitting down.

2. How did Albert help the old man?

3. What does 'a collector' mean? Circle the correct answer.

    (a) A person who collects things.   (b) The things that someone collects.   (c) The hobby of collecting things.

4. How long has Albert collected stamps?

5. Why couldn't Albert buy new stamps?

6. How did the old man thank Albert?

7. Find a word that means 'worth a lot of money'.

F Charlie is doing a project on interesting hobbies.

1

Steve, you make and race model cars. How long have you made model cars?

I've made model cars for six years.

6 years

1998

How long have you raced them?

I've raced them since 1998.

2

Carol, you grow and paint flowers. How long have you grown flowers?

2 years

2003

How long …?

3

Judy, you collect shells and make necklaces. How long …?

4 years

2001

Reading. A world-famous collector.

Bader Yousif Murad has collected model planes since he was 10 years old. Now he is famous because he has the biggest and best collection in the world.

Bader is from the Kingdom of Bahrain, but when he was 10 years old, he lived in the Kingdom of Saudi Arabia. His house was near an airport, and he loved watching the planes. He learnt about all the different planes and which countries they came from.

One day, a kind neighbour gave him a present. It was a toy plane. Bader loved playing with this small plane, and he wanted more planes. Soon he had a collection of planes, but he wanted even more. His parents asked, 'Why do you want so many toys that are all the same?' They gave him books about planes. Bader read the books and learnt a lot.

Bader grew up and got a job at Gulf Air. He also started making model planes. He was very good at making models because he knew so much about planes. Other collectors wanted to buy his models, so in 1998 he started a company called Bader models. Since that year, his company has made model planes and sold them on the Internet. Thousands of people from many countries have bought Bader's models. They all say Bader models are the best in the world.

After 1998, Bader had two jobs. From 7:00 a.m. to 3:00 p.m. he worked at the airport. Then from 3:00 p.m. to midnight, he worked for Bader Models. In 2003, he showed 300 of his models at the Bahrain National Museum. Since then, he has shown them in countries all over the world. He works very hard, but he is happy because he loves his work and he knows his model planes are the best in the world.

Pearson Education Limited
Edinburgh Gate, Harlow,
Essex CM20 2JE
United Kingdom
and Associated Companies throughout the World.

www.longman.com

© Pearson Education Limited 2005

Adaptation copyright © 2004 by Pearson Education Limited
Original edition copyright © Pearson Education Asia Limited 2000
All Rights Reserved.
Published by arrangement with the original publisher,
Pearson Education Asia Limited, a Pearson Education company.

First Published in 2005
Sixth impression 2011

ISBN: 978-1-4058-0267-3

Set in Longman English 14pt
Printed in Malaysia, CTP-PJB
Prepared for the Publishers by Hart McLeod, Cambridge

Photo Acknowledgements

Every effort has been made to trace the copyright holders and we apologise in advance for any unintentional omissions. We would be pleased to insert the appropriate acknowledgement in any subsequent edition of this publication.

We are grateful to the following for permission to reproduce photographs:

Alamy: (cover) (l) (Bill Bachmann); Camera Press: pg99 (ml); Corbis: pg14 (bl) (John D Norman), (br) (James Leynse), pg21 (m), pg28 (r) (Bettmann), pg36 (steam train) (Arthur W V Mace) (Milepost 92 1/2), pg39 (t) (Patrick Ward), (b) (Catherine Karnow), pg42 (Adam Woolfitt), pg56 (tl) (Adam T Woolfitt), pg56 (tr) (Dean Conger), pg84 (t) (Corbis), (b) (Chirstine Fleming), pg99 (bl) (Reuters), pg105 (t) (Peter Wilson), (b) (Charles & Josett Lenars); Digital Vision: (cover) (r) (Royalty Free); DK Images: pg99 (mr); Getty Images: pg36 (dial phone); Imagestate: pg99 (br) (Stephen Myers); Photolibrary.com: pg36 (electric train); Popperfoto: pg36(tl); Powerstock: pg99 (tl) (Superstock), (tr) (age fotostock); PunchStock: (cover) (m) (Royalty Free); Rex: pg21 (t), pg36 (cars and buses), (tall buildings), (mobile phones),

The following photographs were courtesy of:

Qrio robot courtesy of Sony pg70
Roomba courtesy of iRobot pg70
Robots courtesy of Robocup pg70
Bader Yousif Murad (www.badermodels.com) pg126

Picture research by Ann Thomson